DISGUSTING BODILY FUNCTIONS

BY PATRICK PERISH

EPIC

BELLWETHER MEDIA • MINNEAPOLIS, MN

EPIC BOOKS are no ordinary books. They burst with intense action, high-speed heroics, and shadows of the unknown. Are you ready for an Epic adventure?

This edition first published in 2015 by Bellwether Media, Inc.

No part of this publication may be reproduced in whole or in part without written permission of the publisher. For information regarding permission, write to Bellwether Media, Inc., Attention: Permissions Department, 5357 Penn Avenue South, Minneapolis, MN 55419.

Library of Congress Cataloging-in-Publication Data

Perish, Patrick.
  Disgusting bodily functions / by Patrick Perish.
    pages cm. – (Epic. Totally disgusting)
  Summary: "Engaging images accompany information about disgusting bodily functions. The combination of high-interest subject matter and light text is intended for students in grades 2 through 7"– Provided by publisher.
  Audience: Ages 7-12.
  Audience: Grades 2 to 7.
  Includes bibliographical references and index.
  ISBN 978-1-62617-129-9 (hardcover : alk. paper)
  ISBN 978-0-531-27220-6 (paperback : alk. paper)
  1. Human physiology–Juvenile literature. I. Title.
  QP37.P37 2014
  612–dc 3
                         2014004678

Printed in the United States of America, North Mankato, MN.

TABLE OF CONTENTS

EWWW, THE HUMAN BODY!

The human body oozes, stinks, spews, and more. It has the gross factor! But every **repulsive** bodily function has a job to do.

GUNK AND GOO

Gunk builds up at the corners of your eyes while you sleep. This is because your eyes wash away **grime** at night. The tears dry into crusty eye boogers!

STICKY SITUATION

Too much eye gunk can glue eyelids shut. A splash of warm water opens them right up.

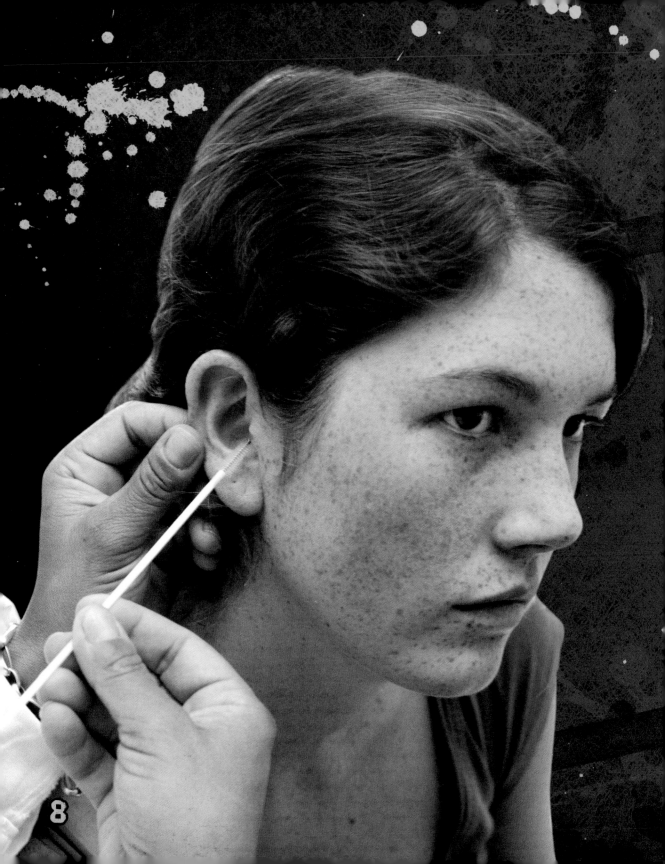

8

Earwax blocks germs and dirt from entering your inner ear. It keeps your ears clean and wet. This orange goop moves with your jaws. Eventually, it dries up and falls out.

← EARWAX

Sort of Disgusting

Totally Disgusting

GROSS-O-METER

9

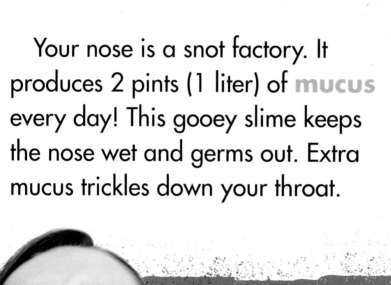

Your nose is a snot factory. It produces 2 pints (1 liter) of **mucus** every day! This gooey slime keeps the nose wet and germs out. Extra mucus trickles down your throat.

Sort of
Disgusting

Totally
Disgusting

GROSS-O-METER

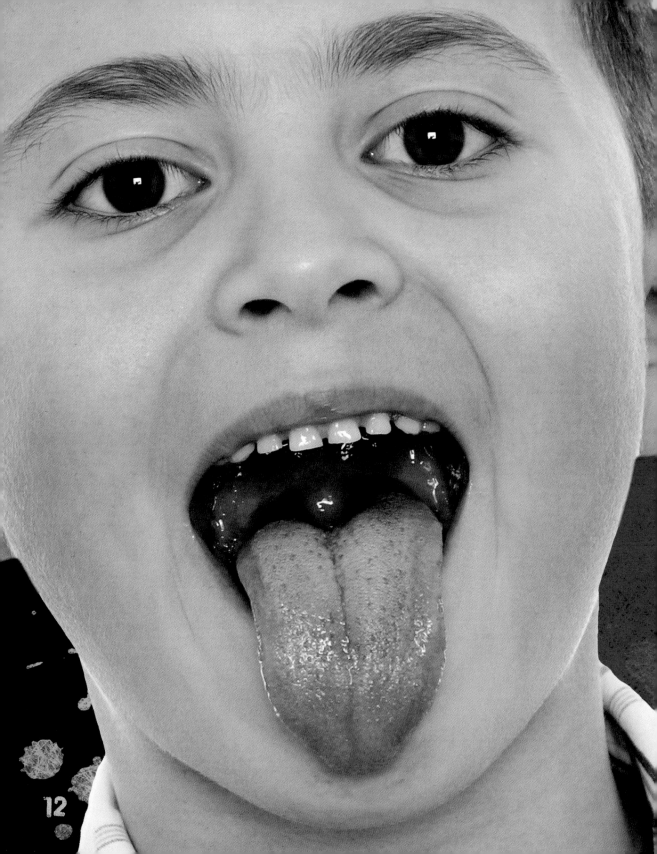

Your mouth oozes 2 to 4 pints (1 to 2 liters) of **saliva** every day! This watery mixture keeps your mouth clean. It also helps break down food.

MOUTHWATERING

You need saliva to taste food. A dry tongue cannot sense flavor.

Sort of Disgusting

Totally Disgusting

GROSS-O-METER

BAD, BAD ODORS

The human body has gas leaks. Gas can build up in the stomach. Then it sometimes bubbles up and leaves the body as a smelly burp.

EXCUSE YOU!

The loudest belch on record was 109 decibels. That is as loud as a jackhammer!

Sort of Disgusting

Totally Disgusting

GROSS-O-METER

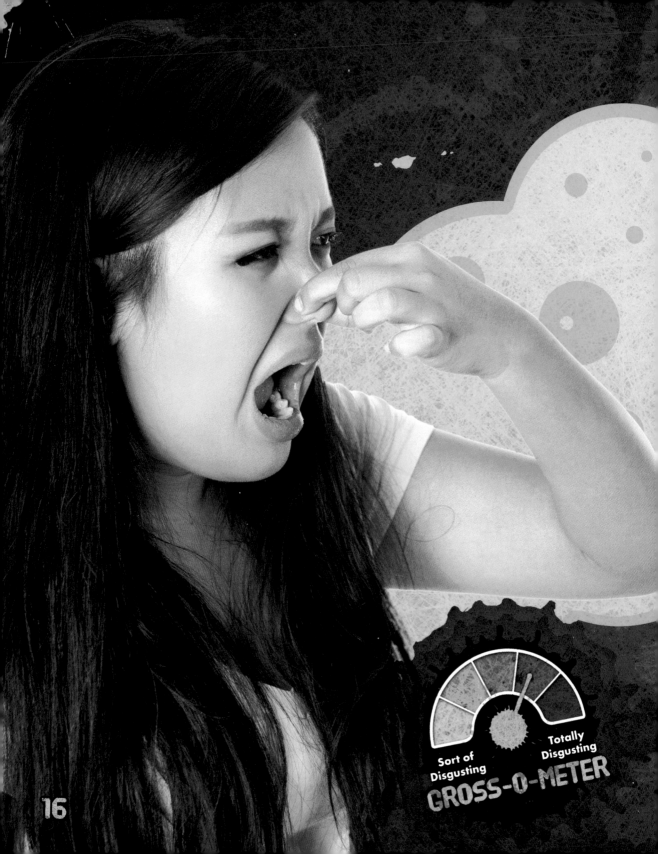

Sort of
Disgusting

Totally
Disgusting

GROSS-O-METER

NATURAL GAS

Most people fart about fifteen times per day.

Gas also exits the body through the other end. Farts happen when your stomach cannot **digest** a food. **Bacteria** turns this food into a horrible stink cloud.

SWEATING AND SPEWING

There is also a gross body
odor from sweat. **Glands** ooze
the oily liquid. Then bacteria make
it stink. Armpits and feet often
smell the worst.

Sometimes the stomach needs to be emptied immediately. You throw up to help out. The **vomit** includes your lunch, **stomach acids**, and mucus. It is just one more nasty function of the human body.

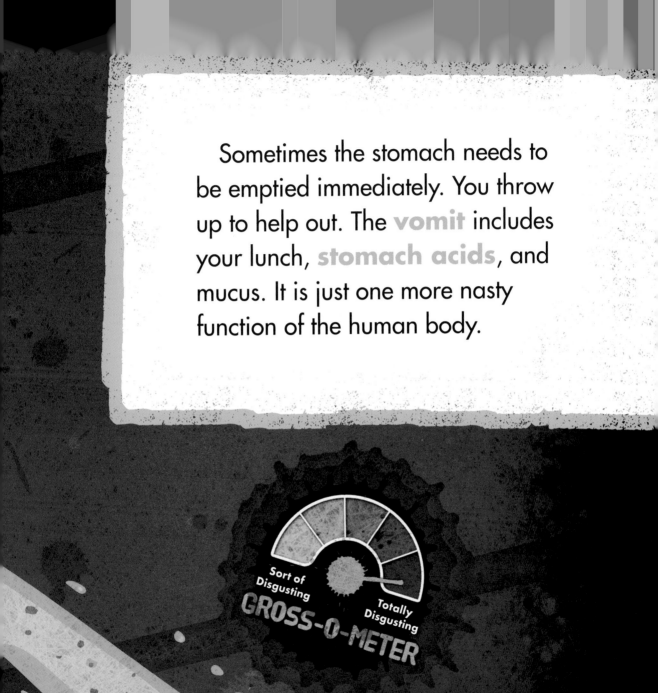

Sort of Disgusting

Totally Disgusting

GROSS-O-METER

GLOSSARY

bacteria—tiny organisms that live everywhere, even inside of us

digest—to break down and get energy from something

earwax—a gooey substance made in the ear

glands—body parts that make substances like sweat and saliva

goop—any kind of oozy, gooey substance

grime—dirt and dust

gunk—any kind of crusty, crumbly substance

inner ear—the part of the human ear that is inside the head

mucus—a sticky substance made in the body; mucus from the nose is also called snot.

odor—strong smell

repulsive—extremely disgusting

saliva—the liquid made in the mouth; saliva is also called spit.

stomach acids—powerful digestive juices that break down food

vomit—a mixture of stomach acids, mucus, and food

TO LEARN MORE

At the Library

Donovan, Sandra. *Hawk & Drool: Gross Stuff in Your Mouth.* Minneapolis, Minn.: Millbrook Press, 2010.

Royston, Angela. *Ooze and Goo.* Chicago, Ill.: Raintree, 2010.

Royston, Angela. *Puke and Poo.* Chicago, Ill.: Raintree, 2010.

On the Web

Learning more about disgusting bodily functions is as easy as 1, 2, 3.

1. Go to www.factsurfer.com.

2. Enter "disgusting bodily functions" into the search box.

3. Click the "Surf" button and you will see a list of related web sites.

With factsurfer.com, finding more information

INDEX

The images in this book are reproduced through the courtesy of: PathDoc, front cover (top left), pp. 5, 16; Roblan, front cover (top right); sdominick, front cover (bottom), Scholastic cover, p. 10; Daniele Pietrobelli, p. 5 (top right); DWaschnig, p. 5 (middle right); UpperCut Images/ SuperStock, p. 5 (bottom right); Jon Eppard, p. 7; Burger/ Phanie/ SuperStock, p. 8; has2006, p. 11; Maksim Striganov, p. 12; Kamira, p. 15; Armin Staudt, p. 17; Mareen Fischinger/ Getty Images, p. 18; Carlos Yudica, p. 19; Rob Lewine/ Tetra Images/ Corbis, p. 20.